The Blue Day Book

A Lesson in Cheering Yourself Up

Bradley Trevor Greive

**Andrews McMeel
Publishing, LLC**

Kansas City • Sydney • London

10 11 12 13 14 WKT 10 9 8 7 6 5 4 3 2 1

ISBN-10: 0-7407-9374-8
ISBN-13: 978-0-7407-9374-5

Book design by Holly Camerlinck
Images hand coloured by Tim Clift

Photo Credits
Corbis Australia Pty Ltd www.corbis.com
Getty Images www.gettyimages.com
Photolibrary www.photolibrary.com
Emerald City Images www.emeraldcityimages.com.au
D. Robert Franz www.franzfoto.com
© **Frans Lanting** www.lanting.com

Credit details for the remarkable photographers whose work appears
in *The Blue Day Book* and other books by Bradley Trevor Greive
are freely available at www.btgstudios.com.

Attention: Schools and Businesses
Andrews McMeel books are available at quantity discounts with bulk purchase for educational,
business, or sales promotional use. For information, please write to: Special Sales Department,
Andrews McMeel Publishing, LLC, 1130 Walnut Street, Kansas City, Missouri 64106.

To my wonderful parents, Fay and Trevor Greive,
who never stopped taking me out to see the world
even after I was bitten by penguins, three times.

Foreword

I have always had great affection for animals of all shapes and sizes, with a particularly soft spot for frogs. I like their spongy tummies and oh-so-sensitive toes. I like their delicate skin that feels like moist, refrigerated velvet, and I love the way their large luminous eyes stare at the world with an unfettered sense of wonder. I especially enjoy listening to frogs celebrate the arrival of rain with a yodeled belching of raucous throat music, calling our attention to the fact that life has been renewed. Maybe this froggy fascination stems from living in Australia, where water is so precious that frogs have become proxy ambassadors of good fortune, or perhaps deep down I'm just like so many little boys who never really grew up. Opinions vary.

Nevertheless, if you had told me that a frog would one day change my life, I would never have believed you. Yet that is exactly what happened. Looking back to 1998, when I first fell for the grumpy blue face that now adorns the cover of *The Blue Day Book,* I still find it hard to comprehend the extraordinary impact this little edition has had on my life and how it has reached into the hearts and homes of so many people throughout the world.

The Blue Day Book's conception was hardly immaculate, though certainly honest. On the day I first dreamed up this little book, I was living and working in grunge-chic squalor in a seedy loft located directly opposite the largest railway station in Australia. Whenever a train arrived or departed, roughly every ten seconds or so, my apartment shuddered like a sick dog, various high-velocity vermin scurried about, and termite snow rained down upon me. To make matters worse, I was fiscally impaled, romantically dislocated, and I had caught a terrible flu during the coldest, wettest winter I can remember. I was not a happy camper.

Rummaging desperately through all my pockets for loose change, I discovered I had enough money to catch a taxi into town, enjoy a movie, or eat a hot meal—but sadly, not all three. Braving the rain, I slid spinelessly into a greasy spoon, ordered a burger, and began to scribble my tortured feelings on a paper napkin. I wrote some rather bad poetry, none of it worth mentioning except one particular line that stood out in my mind:

"The world turns grey and I grow tired."

I wrote this line again and again, and even illustrated it with an exhausted tortoise collapsed helplessly on its back. It seemed to be the perfect metaphor for how I felt at that exact moment. After nine years and seven unpublished books, I had nothing at all to show for my labours except a huge pile of rejection letters. I felt beaten, defeated. All the colour had faded from view, and I was too tired and humiliated to take another step.

I wallowed in the pungent pudding of self-pity for a time, and then it struck me how interesting it would be if the world really *were* devoid of colour. Imagine if we saw only black, white, and shades of grey. It soon occurred to me that this was actually how many animals, especially dogs, see the world all the time, and they don't seem too depressed about it. Before I knew it, I was smiling, and the smile became a chuckle as I remembered all the hilarious black-and-white animal photos I had seen in *Life* magazine when I was growing up in Singapore. Pretty soon I realized I was taking myself and my setbacks far too seriously. No matter how tough things were, at least I was doing what I most wanted to do. I had a lot to be grateful for and a great deal to look forward to. *The Blue Day Book* was born.

I have many people to thank for the creative freedom I now enjoy. Beloved members of my extended publishing family and numerous talented photographers and designers are often mentioned in the acknowledgements of my books, but at this point, I really want to thank you, the reader, for giving me a chance. I had no idea so many people would enjoy the same slightly twisted perspectives that I do, or that they would see themselves and their loved ones in each of the incredible animal photographs as I have (I used to relate most to the bear cub on page 18, although these days I feel closer and closer to the cat on page 27). It gives me great joy to think of how many people giggle or sigh at the same thoughts that have moved me to laughter and tears, and it makes me feel very positive about our collective future because something so simple, and frankly a little silly at times, can bring us together for a moment to reflect on what matters most.

The success of *The Blue Day Book* has certainly changed my life and, I'm glad to say, a few other lives as well. Proceeds from this series now support at least one major conservation project on every continent, preserving all manner of endangered species, including Malayan sun bears and Burmese roof turtles in Asia, brown bears in Russia, okapi and painted hunting dogs in Africa, numerous exotic Australian mammals, and yes, even a couple of rare and precious frogs. For me, there are so many special memories and feelings wrapped up in *The Blue Day Book* that I merely have to look at my little amphibious friend on the cover, and it makes me smile. I sincerely hope this special tenth-anniversary edition makes you smile, too.

March 2010

The Blue Day Book

Everybody has blue days.

These are miserable days when you feel lousy,

grumpy,

lonely,

and utterly exhausted.

Days when you feel small and insignificant,

when everything seems just out of reach.

You can't rise to the occasion.

Just getting started seems impossible.

On blue days you can become paranoid
that everyone is out to get you.
(This is not always such a bad thing.)

You feel frustrated and anxious,

which can induce a nail-biting frenzy

that can escalate into a triple-chocolate-mud-cake-
eating frenzy in the blink of an eye!

On blue days you feel like you're floating
in an ocean of sadness.

You're about to burst into tears at any moment
and you don't even know why.

Ultimately, you feel like you're wandering through life without purpose.

You're not sure how much longer
you can hang on,

and you feel like shouting,
'Will someone please shoot me!'

It doesn't take much to bring on a blue day.

You might just wake up
not feeling or looking your best,

find some new wrinkles,

put on a little weight,

or get a huge pimple on your nose.

You could forget your date's name

or have an embarrassing photograph published.

You might get dumped, divorced, or fired,

make a fool of yourself in public,

be afflicted with a demeaning nickname,

or just have a plain old bad-hair day.

Maybe work is a pain in the bum.

You're under serious pressure
to fill someone else's shoes,

your boss is picking on you,

and everyone in the office
is driving you mad.

You might have a splitting headache,

or a slipped disk,

bad breath,

a toothache,

chronic gas,

dry lips,

or a nasty ingrown toenail.

Whatever the reason, you're convinced
that someone up there doesn't like you.

Oh, what to do, what to dooo?

Well, if you're like most people, you'll hide behind a flimsy belief that everything will sort itself out.

Then you'll spend the rest of your life
looking over your shoulder, waiting for everything
to go wrong all over again.

All the while becoming crusty and cynical

or a pathetic, snivelling victim,

until you get so depressed that you lie down
and beg the earth to swallow you up

or, even worse, become addicted
to Billy Joel songs.

This is crazy, because you're only young once

and you're never old twice.

Who knows what fantastic things are in store
just around the corner?

After all, the world is full
of amazing discoveries,

things you can't even imagine right now.

There are delicious, happy sniffs,

and scrumptious snacks to share.

Hey, you might end up fabulously rich

or even become a huge superstar (one day).

Sounds good, doesn't it?

But wait, there's more!

There are handstands

and games to play

and yoga

and karaoke

and wild, crazy, bohemian dancing.

But best of all, there's romance.

Which means long dreamy stares,

whispering sweet nothings,

cuddles,

smooches,

more smooches,

and even more smooches,

a frisky love bite or two,

and then, well, anything goes.

So how can you find that blissful
'just sliding into a hot bubble bath'
kind of feeling?

It's easy.

First, stop slinking away from all those nagging issues.
It's time to face the music.

Now, just relax. Take some deep breaths
(in through the nose and out through the mouth).
Try to meditate if you can.

Or go for a walk to clear your head.

Accept the fact that you'll have to let go
of some emotional baggage.

Try seeing things from a different perspective.

Maybe you're actually the one at fault.
If that's the case, be big enough to say you're sorry
(it's never too late to do this).

If someone else is doing the wrong thing,
stand up tall and say, 'That's not right and I won't
stand for it!' It's okay to be forceful.

(It's rarely okay to blow raspberries.)

Be proud of who you are,

but don't lose the ability to laugh at yourself.

(This is a lot easier when you associate
with positive people.)

Live every day as if it were your last,
because one day it will be.

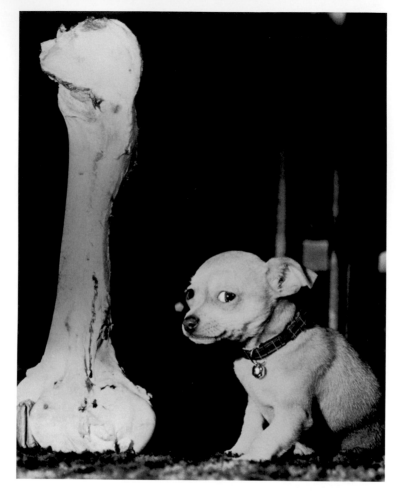

Don't be afraid to bite off
more than you can chew.

Take big risks.

Never hang back. Get out there and go for it.

After all, isn't that what life is all about?

I think so too.

Bradley Trevor Greive

Since the debut of his bestseller *The Blue Day Book*, Bradley Trevor Greive has become an international publishing sensation. His books have sold more than 20 million copies in 115 countries. A former Australian paratrooper, BTG left the army to pursue creative misadventure. Between qualifying as a cosmonaut for the Russian space program and writing books, BTG seeks out wildlife and wild places, and has even been kissed by a walrus. However, he has also been bitten by penguins, bear cubs, rabid monkeys, and giant bats. To add insult to injury, he was slapped in the face by a sea turtle, suffers greatly from cat allergies, and was almost killed by a guinea pig. He spends most of his time in a tiny Tasmanian hamlet with his three Great Danes.